Intro to
Bear Hunting
For Kids

Frank W Koretum

Table of Contents

Introduction to Bear Hunting.. 3

The History of Bear Hunting... 4

Bear Characteristics 6

Bear Regulations... 8

Safety... 9

Clothing... 12

Additional Gear... 15

Food to Pack 19

Firearms for Bear Hunting 21

Shotguns for Bear Hunting... 24

Bows for Bear Hunting 26

Seasons to Hunt Bear 28

When to Bear Hunt 30

Weather 33

Where to Hunt.. 36

Scouting... 39

Bear Decoys... 41

Calling Bear... 43

Methods 44

The Environment and You 56

Recap.. 58

Introduction to Bear Hunting

Are you ready to learn how to go hunting for bears? This book will show you the way! Going hunting for bears can be an incredibly exciting and rewarding experience, no matter your age. It's a great way to get out in nature and explore the wilderness. Plus, hunting bear provides kids with a unique opportunity to hone their tracking and hunting skills. With this book, you'll learn all the ins-and-outs of hunting bear: from choosing the right kinds of gear to proper preparation and safety tips. And once you've mastered these basics, we'll take you on some real hunts – complete with helpful strategies so you can start catching your own bear!

So what are you waiting for?

Let's get started on this bear hunting adventure!

The History of Bear Hunting

Bear hunting is an activity that has been around for centuries, with the first recorded hunting of bear occurring in North America in 1620. The practice of hunting bear was originally used by Native Americans and early settlers as a way to provide food and clothing. But over time hunting bear has evolved into a sport enjoyed by many people today who are looking for the challenge of hunting a large and powerful animal.

Hunting bear became more popular in the United States during the 19th century when many states began requiring hunting licenses. With this increase in hunting, there was also an increase in conservation efforts to ensure that populations wouldn't be depleted by excessive hunting. These efforts led to some regulations on hunting bear such as limits on bag limits, hunting seasons, and hunting areas.

There are a variety of methods used for hunting bear, including baiting and still hunting. Baiting involves setting up bait to attract the bear and then waiting for them to come to the bait so you can take a shot with your hunting rifle or bow. Still hunting involves slowly moving through an area looking for signs of bear such as tracks or scat before taking a shot at the animal. Both methods require knowledge of the terrain, patience and good marksmanship skills in order to be successful.

Bear hunting is dangerous but there are a few steps that can be taken to increase safety while hunting bear. The first step is to make sure you have proper training in hunting safety and bear hunting techniques. It is also important to make sure that you are wearing the proper clothing and equipment such as warm clothes, hunting boots, and a hunting knife in case of an emergency. Finally, it is essential to stay aware of your surroundings at all times while hunting bear to make sure that you don't get into any dangerous situations.

Bear hunting can be an exciting and rewarding activity but it is important to take the necessary steps to ensure that you do it safely. With the right training, preparation, and safety measures in place bear hunting can be a great experience for hunters of all ages. With knowledge comes power so make sure you have the right information before going out on your next hunting trip!

Bear Characteristics

In order to be successful at hunting bear, it is important to have a good understanding of what they look like, where they are found in the United States, their habits and behaviors, and other useful information that can help you locate them in the wild.

Bears come in many shapes, sizes and colors. They are identified by either black or brown fur depending on the species. The American Black Bear has a coat color ranging from yellowish-brown to black while the Brown Bear has shades of brown fur consisting mostly of shades of cinnamon, dark chocolate brown and sandy blonde. Both bear species usually weigh between 250-600 pounds with males being larger than females. They can grow up to 8 feet tall and live for 25-30 years in the wild.

The types of habitats that bear prefer depend on the region but generally they are found in deciduous, coniferous or mixed forests with access to rivers, streams, lakes or ponds. Bear are also spotted in mountainous regions where there is thick vegetation and a plentiful supply of food sources such as berries, nuts, insects and small animals.

When hunting bear it is important to be able to distinguish them from other animals like deer which they may share similarities with. One way to tell them apart is their size; bear are large compared to deer or other animals in the same habitat. Another distinguishing feature of bear is their sense of smell and sight. Bears have a very strong sense of smell which enables them to detect food from up to 20 miles away, while their eyesight is not as sharp compared to other animals. They are also incredibly good at detecting movement and can pick up on even the slightest motion in their surroundings.

In conclusion, hunting bear requires knowledge of their appearance, habitat and habits to be successful. Being familiar with what they look like, the types of food they eat, their average size and weight, where they are found in the US and how to distinguish them from other animals is key for a successful hunting adventure.

Bear Regulations

Bears have long been a popular hunting game in the United States, and their hunting regulations differ by state. As such, it's important to understand the regulations for bear hunting before you begin hunting. In general, most states set specific times of year when bears can be hunted and restrictions on age or sex that can be taken. Additionally, each state has a daily limit – how many bears one person is allowed to harvest per day – as well as a possession limit – which is the total number of bears you are allowed to possess from hunting today plus any you already have at home.

Most states require hunters to purchase hunting licenses prior to hunting bear; however some states allow hunting below certain ages without requiring a license, or offer free hunting licenses as a way to get young people into hunting activities.

Daily limits are the maximum number of bear that one person is allowed to harvest per day within the state's hunting season. Possession limits are the total number of bear you are allowed to have in your possession from hunting today plus any additional bears you may already have at home.

Possession limits differ by state and often depend on whether it is an archery-only season, or general hunting season, but generally speaking most states only allow hunters to take one bear per year. In some cases, states will also operate a lottery system where hunters must apply for limited numbers of "bear tags" that can be used during hunting seasons.

In conclusion, hunting bear can be a rewarding experience that brings us closer to nature. However, it's important for hunters to familiarize themselves with the hunting regulations specific to their state before they go hunting in order to ensure that they are hunting responsibly and legally. Additionally, all hunters should be aware of daily limits and possession limits as well as any requirements regarding hunting licenses or applications for bear tags prior to hunting season.

Safety

When hunting for bears, it is of the utmost importance that you do so safely. Hunting can be dangerous due to many factors, such as unsafe hunting tools and being unprepared for the outdoors. It is essential to understand the risks of hunting before going out in search of a bear. This section will explain some of those risks and ways to minimize them when hunting for bears.

When hunting a bear, it is important to use the right tool for the job; this means having a hunting knife, gun, or bow ready when out searching for a bear. As with any hunting weapon, there are safety measures that should always be taken into account when handling such weapons - these include proper storage and safety testing before hunting. It is also important to use the hunting tool properly, as improper handling can lead to dangerous situations.

Another risk when hunting for a bear is getting lost in the wilderness while tracking it. This can be an extremely dangerous situation, so it is essential to have a plan of where you are going and how you will get back if necessary. A GPS device or paper map and compass can be helpful in navigating your way through any terrain, but if these devices become unavailable then knowing some basic orienteering skills may be necessary.

When hunting for bears, there are risks of getting injured by the animal itself if hunting without proper safety measures in place. There are also risks of physical injury from falling from hunting stands, hunting blinds, or other hunting structures. It is important to make sure these hunting structures are stable and secure before using them. Wearing the right safety equipment, such as hunting gloves and boots, can help protect you if an unexpected situation should arise while hunting.

Weather conditions can also be a risk when hunting for bears; inclement weather can lead to dangerous situations due to slippery terrain or low visibility. It is important to check the weather forecast before heading out and come prepared with the proper clothing and gear for any kind of weather condition that may arise.

Hunting safety is paramount when hunting for a bear. To ensure your safety while hunting, it is highly recommended that you take a hunting education course. In most states, hunting safety classes are required after a certain age, but they can often be taken online as well. Even if hunting education classes are not mandated in your state, taking one can help you stay safe when hunting for bear and other wildlife. Ultimately, hunting safety should always be taken seriously to reduce any risks while hunting.

This information will provide an overview of the importance of safety when bear hunting and some of the things that can be dangerous when hunting including a hunting knives, guns, bows, getting lost, getting injured in the woods (including falling from hunting stands), getting injured by the bears you are hunting and inclement weather with ways to avoid these risks. Taking hunting education classes can help you stay safe when hunting for bear and other wildlife. Remember to always take hunting safety seriously, so you can enjoy the sport of hunting with no worry!

Clothing

When hunting, it is important to stay as hidden and undetected as possible. Camouflage hunting clothing can help you do this by breaking up your silhouette and blending in with your environment. There are several different pieces of hunting apparel that should be worn for bear hunting.

Layering your clothing is essential when hunting during cold weather conditions. It allows you to wear multiple layers of camouflage hunting clothing to break up your outline, while also providing some warmth from the outside elements. Start with a base layer such as a lightweight long sleeve shirt or t-shirt made out of moisture wicking material like merino wool or polyester, then add an insulation layer such as a fleece jacket or hunting vest. Finally, add a hunting jacket or hunting coat that uses a waterproof breathable membrane to prevent moisture from getting in while still allowing vapor to escape.

Your hunting boots should match the environment you're hunting in and keep your foot dry and comfortable. Choose insulated hunting boots with a thick rubber sole if hunting in cold weather conditions, or opt for lightweight hunting boots during warmer months. It is also important to wear an ankle support boot for added stability when tracking game over uneven terrain.

It doesn't matter how well blended into the environment your clothing is if your face stands out like a sore thumb! Camouflage face masks are essential for bear hunters because they help to break up your facial outline and keep you hidden from the bear's sight. Choose a hunting face mask that is waterproof, breathable, and has adjustable straps for additional comfort.

Your hunting hat should be lightweight with an adjustable chin strap for a secure fit in case of windy conditions. Choose a hunting cap with built-in camouflage fabric as well as UPF sun protection so you can stay out hunting all day long without worrying about sunburns or UV rays.

Bear hunting requires having the right clothing to stay hidden while hunting in the outdoors. This includes wearing layers of warm camouflage clothes, hunting boots, a camouflage face mask, and a camouflage hat so you remain hidden in your hunting environment. All of these pieces of hunting apparel are essential for a successful hunting experience. With the right clothing and hunting gear, you'll be sure to bag a bear!

Additional Gear

It's important to be prepared for bear hunting. When selecting the gear you take with, it's essential to choose wisely. You'll need your hunting weapon, of course, but there are many other items that can help you have a successful hunting experience hunting bears. From binoculars and range finders to fire starters and backpacks, read on to learn what additional gear is best for bear hunting.

Binoculars:

One of the most essential items when hunting bears is a good set of binoculars. Binoculars will help you get a better view of far away objects so you can spot potential game before getting too close or spooking them away. Make sure to select a pair with a wide field of view and good resolution. Having a pair of binoculars on you at all times will help you spot potential hunting opportunities from afar.

Range Finder:

Another item to consider when hunting bears is a rangefinder. This device measures the distance between two points, allowing hunters to know exactly how far away their targets are from them. Rangefinders come in various sizes and features, so it's important to select one that suits your hunting needs best.

Hunting Knife:

A hunting knife is also essential for bear hunting. You'll want something with a secure grip and sharp blade that can be used for skinning animals or cutting through brush so you can move more quietly without being heard by bears. Look for hunting knives with ergonomic handles and designed to be used in the outdoors.

Multitool:

Having a multitool such as a Leatherman can also be useful when hunting bears. A multitool is a small device that contains multiple tools in one, such as pliers, screwdrivers, bottle openers, and more. Having one of these on hand will help you tackle any unexpected repairs or problems you may encounter while hunting bears.

Compass:

A compass is another essential item to bring along on bear hunting trips. Knowing which direction you are facing can make all the difference in finding your prey quickly and easily. Choose a good quality compass that features clear markings and an adjustable dial so you can easily read it no matter the lighting.

Fire Starter:

When hunting bears, having a reliable fire starter can be a lifesaver. During cold weather hunting trips, you'll need a source of heat to stay warm and cook food, so bringing along fire starters is essential. Select one that will light quickly in any conditions and has enough fuel to get your fire going for hours at a time.

First Aid Kit:

Another must-have item when hunting bear is a first aid kit. Accidents can happen while hunting, so it's important to always have medical supplies on hand just in case of an emergency. Make sure your first aid kit contains all the necessary items such as bandages, antiseptic, tweezers, and more.

Flashlight or Headlamp:

A flashlight or headlamp is also important for hunting bears. These devices will help you see in dark areas or at night, making it easier to spot game. Make sure the one you choose is bright enough and has a long battery life so you don't have to worry about running out of light while hunting.

Backpack:

Finally, bringing along a sturdy backpack can come in handy when hunting bear. Select one with plenty of pockets and compartments so you can easily store all your hunting gear, including your weapon. Look for backpacks that are designed specifically for hunting trips and have features such as waterproofing and padding to protect your items from the elements.

By following these tips, you'll be sure to have all the necessary hunting gear when hunting bear. Remember to stay safe and enjoy your hunting trip!

Food to Pack

When hunting bear, it is important to bring food that will provide you with enough energy and hydration to last the entire day. Packing the right kind of food can make all the difference in having a successful hunting trip.

Sandwiches are a great option for bear hunting because they are easy to put together and provide protein and carbohydrates for sustained energy throughout the day. Use high-protein ingredients such as meats, cheeses, eggs, nuts, and beans for your sandwich fillings. This will give you an extra boost of energy that will be beneficial when hunting bear in remote areas.

Beef jerky is another excellent source of protein for hunting bear. It is high in protein and low in fat, which makes it a great snack to have on hand. Plus, jerky is easy to store and doesn't take up much room in your hunting bag.

Fruits and nuts are great sources of natural energy that will give you the fuel you need for hunting bear all day long. Pack some fresh fruits such as apples, oranges, or bananas for an extra burst of energy when you need it most. For nuts, almonds and cashews are especially good because they contain magnesium which can help keep your muscles from cramping throughout the day.

When hunting bear, hydration is key! Bring plenty of water with you, as well as energy drinks if desired. This will help keep you feeling energized and ready for hunting all day long.

When hunting bear, it is important to pack the right kind of food. Sandwiches, beef jerky, fruits, nuts, and plenty of water are all essential for providing sustenance throughout the hunting day. With these snacks in your hunting bag, you'll have plenty of energy and hydration to last until dark!

Firearms for Bear Hunting

Caliber is an important factor in hunting, especially when hunting bears. It can help determine how effective your hunting will be and how far away you can shoot accurately. The caliber of a rifle indicates the size of the bullet used by that rifle. Generally speaking, the larger the caliber, the more powerful and potentially more accurate it is. But there are trade-offs; higher calibers tend to have more recoil (kickback) which can make them harder to handle for beginning hunters. Below we will discuss different calibers from lowest to highest and what range they might be able to effectively hunt at as well as adding a scope or not and why this may be beneficial for bear hunting.

.22 caliber: This is the smallest and weakest hunting rifle available, but it is still a popular hunting gun for smaller animals like rabbits and squirrels. The range at which this gun can effectively hunt is relatively short, only about 50 yards due to its low power. It is a good choice for younger or beginning hunters learning the basics of hunting since there's not much kickback when you fire and it will help them get used to handling a rifle before moving up in caliber size.

.243 Winchester: A step up from the .22 caliber, this round offers more power and accuracy over longer distances than its smaller counterpart. It has an effective hunting range of around 100 yards which makes it suitable for hunting medium-sized game such as deer or antelope. It also produces less recoil than larger calibers so it may be easier for beginner hunters to handle.

.308 Winchester: This is the most popular hunting caliber in the United States and is an excellent choice for hunting medium-sized animals like deer, elk, and moose. It has a hunting range of about 200 yards and can even be used to hunt bear depending on the situation. The downside is that this rifle has more kickback than smaller calibers which can make it difficult for beginners to handle at first.

30-06 Springfield: This large caliber round is one of the most powerful hunting rounds available and can effectively take down large animals like bears over long distances (up to 500 yards). It has significant recoil so it's not recommended for inexperienced hunters. Adding a scope to this rifle can help increase accuracy and hunting range, making it more effective for hunting bear.

By understanding the different calibers available, you can decide which one is best suited to your hunting needs. Smaller calibers have less kickback but are only suitable for hunting small animals over short distances while larger calibers offer more power and longer hunting ranges but also generate more recoil when fired. Adding a scope to your rifle can make a big difference in terms of accuracy and hunting range as well. Ultimately, it's important to choose the right caliber based on your hunting preferences and skill level; if you're hunting bear, a larger caliber like the 30-06 Springfield may be your best bet. Keep these points in mind and you'll be ready for your next bear hunting trip! Good luck and happy hunting!

Shotguns for Bear Hunting

When hunting bear, it is important to understand the different gauges of shotguns and how they can affect your hunting experience. The most common shotgun gauges are 12, 20, 28 and .410. The lower the number of gauge a shotgun has, the more powerful it will be with less recoil; this means that shots from a 12-gauge shotgun will have more power than those from a .410 gauge. With that in mind, as a beginner or younger hunter you should start out with something like a 20-gauge for hunting bear until you grow accustomed to larger guns which would then allow you to move up to a 12-gauge.

Shotguns for hunting bear are typically loaded with slugs rather than bird shot. Slugs are single large bullets which provide greater power and accuracy when hunting larger game, such as bear, than bird shot does. Bird shot is made up of small pellets which is best for hunting birds.

The type of shotgun you use can also make a difference in your hunting experience. Pump action shotguns require the user to manually load the next round before being able to fire again, while semi-automatic shotguns automatically load the next round allowing for faster firing with less effort on the part of the hunter.

When hunting bear it is important to understand both the gauge and type of shotgun that would be suitable for such a hunting expedition. Shotguns loaded with slugs provide greater power and accuracy when hunting larger game while pump action and semi-automatic shotguns can be used to increase the speed at which a hunter is able to fire their gun. It is usually recommended that beginners or younger hunters start with something like a 20 gauge until they gain more experience and become accustomed to handling larger guns. Ultimately, when hunting bear the type of shotgun and gauge selected will depend on a variety of factors such as hunting experience and personal preference.

Bows for Bear Hunting

Bow hunting is a challenging, but rewarding activity that requires patience and practice. When hunting bear, it's important to choose the right type of bow for the job. The three main types of hunting bows are longbows, recurve bows and compound bows.

Longbows have been around since ancient times, and they remain popular hunting tools today. Longbows are made from wood or laminated wood/fiberglass materials and shoot arrows further than wood. They offer good accuracy up to 30 yards away, but beyond that distance shooting with a longbow becomes difficult. Longbows require a significant amount of arm strength to draw them back in order to fire an arrow effectively.

Recurve bows have a curved shape that allows them to store more energy than longbows. This gives recurve bows the ability to shoot arrows further and with more accuracy, making them ideal hunting tools for distances between 20-40 yards. They come in wooden or fiberglass materials and require less arm strength than a longbow.

Compound bows are the most powerful hunting bow type available today. Compound bows use pulleys and cables to store energy which makes it easier to draw back the bowstring, allowing significantly greater arrow speed and power. This makes compound bows effective hunting weapons from distances of up to 50 yards away.

No matter what kind of hunting bow you choose, it takes practice and dedication in order to become proficient at hunting with it. It's important to practice hunting regularly in order to increase accuracy and distance shooting capabilities.

When hunting, it's also important to choose the right type of arrow head for the job. Broadheads are designed for hunting large game such as bear, while field points are better suited for target shooting and hunting small game animals. Different arrow shaft types can also affect a bow's performance. Wood arrows work well with recurve bows but may not provide enough power when hunting large animals, while carbon arrows are lightweight yet strong and offer good penetration on larger animals.

In conclusion, hunting bear requires the right equipment and practice in order to be successful. Choosing between longbows, recurves, and compound bows depends on the hunting distance and desired accuracy, as well as personal preference. Different arrowhead types and shafts can also affect hunting performance. With dedication and practice, hunting bear with a bow can be an incredibly rewarding experience.

Seasons to Hunt Bear

It's important to know the different times of year when hunting is legal, as well as what techniques are most effective during each part of hunting season. In this section, we will discuss the different times of year for bear hunting, how to determine which season is best for hunting, and the techniques that will be most effective during each part of hunting season.

Early bear hunting season typically begins in the fall months, with hunting often taking place between August and October. The early season is an ideal time to hunt because the bears are typically still active in preparation for the winter. Some of the most successful techniques during this part of hunting season include stalking and baiting with bait such as fruit, nuts, or honey. It can also be beneficial to use a decoy to attract bears closer for a better view.

Once the winter months arrive, hunting bears can get a bit more challenging as they become less active and their fur begins to thin out. Mid season hunting typically takes place between December and February, with hunting often taking place on days when temperatures are warmer and the snow is not too deep. During this part of hunting season, it is important to focus on areas that have thicker vegetation as bear retreat to these areas for warmth. The most successful techniques during this time include calling and tracking, which requires a sharp eye since tracks can be hard to detect in deeper snow.

As spring approaches, bear hunting begins to pick back up again with late season hunting occurring between March and May. Bears are more active during this time as they begin to wake up from hibernation and search for food. Late season hunting can be tricky, however, since bears have thinned out fur and are usually in small groups or alone. Some of the best techniques during late season hunting include tracking fresh scents and using scent glands to attract nearby bears.

Bear hunting can be a fun and exciting experience when done properly. Knowing which season is best for hunting, as well as what techniques will be most effective during each part of hunting season is essential. By following the tips outlined above, you will increase your chances of success on your hunt!

When to Bear Hunt

With the right knowledge and preparation, hunting bears can be an enjoyable experience that can yield the rewards of providing sustenance for your family or just a good time out in nature. But it's important to understand when bear hunting is best done and what techniques work best depending on the time of day, as this will increase your chances of success significantly. Let's look at hunting during morning, afternoon and sunset to see how you can get the most out of each type of hunt.

The early morning hours are often considered some of the best times to go bear hunting, especially ½ hour before sunrise up until mid-morning. This is because the bears are often searching for food and water during these hours, making them more active and easier to spot. To hunt successfully in the morning, use a hunting blind or find a tree with good visibility that you can sit in and wait for a bear to come near. You'll want to be as quiet as possible so that your presence doesn't scare away any potential targets. It's also important to use scent blockers or hunting lures to attract nearby bears, increasing your chances of success.

The afternoon is usually slower when hunting bear but can still be effective. To hunt during the daytime, use hunting calls and decoys to draw bears out of their dens and into hunting grounds. You'll want to make sure you're hunting in areas with good visibility as this will give you an advantage when spotting a bear before it spots you. It's also a good idea to pay attention to wind direction so that your scent doesn't carry too far and alert any nearby bears.

The last few hours of sunlight are usually the best time for hunting bear due to decreased activity among other wildlife species, making them easier targets for hunters. During these times, use tree stands or hunting blinds with camouflage coverings to conceal your presence from the animals while providing enough light to spot potential targets. You may also want to consider hunting from a distance with the aid of bait piles. This method allows you to hunt without being detected, but also requires some practice and skill in order to be successful.

Bear hunting can be a rewarding experience whether done during morning, afternoon or sunset. It's important to understand when hunting is best done and what techniques work best for each time of day so that you can increase your chances of success. In the morning, use hunting blinds or trees with good visibility and scent blockers or hunting lures. During the afternoon, use hunting calls and lures in areas with good visibility and pay attention to wind direction as well. At sunset, use tree stands or hunting blinds with camouflage coverings while hunting from a distance with the aid of bait piles. With the right knowledge, bear hunting can be an enjoyable activity that provides sustenance for your family or just a good time out in nature.

Weather

As with all hunting, the right conditions and techniques can vastly improve your chances of success in bear hunting. In this section, we will explore different weather conditions that are favorable for bear hunting and discuss the most effective techniques in each situation.

On sunny days, bears tend to be more active during the day and remain awake longer than on overcast days or colder days, making them easier to hunt. Bears also become accustomed to their environment when it is sunny out and leverage their keen sense of smell and hearing to look for food sources such as berries or small animals. To take advantage of this, hunting from high points such as a tree stand or elevated blind can be very effective. The sun also helps you spot bears far away and provides enough light to shoot accurately with firearms or bows. It is important to keep in mind the wind direction when hunting on sunny days, as bears have a very sensitive sense of smell - if you don't account for the wind, they may detect you before you are able to hunt them.

On overcast days, it can be much harder to spot bears due to the lack of sunlight, however hunting during these conditions can still be successful depending on the techniques used. On overcast days, it can be more beneficial to focus your hunting efforts around food sources, as bears may be more focused on hunting for food than they would be during sunny days. Setting baits in areas where bears are likely to frequent can be very effective on overcast days - the bait will attract the bear and you can use a blind nearby to remain undetected while hunting.

On cold days, hunting is usually more successful due to the fact that bears become sluggish in colder temperatures and spend most of their time sleeping or looking for shelter. As a result, hunting from elevated stands or blinds near den sites is often very successful, as bears may not even notice your presence until it's too late. Additionally, since hunting from a stand or blind requires sitting still for extended periods of time, hunting on cold days can be much more comfortable with the right gear or an enclosed stand and less energy intensive than hunting on hot or sunny days.

On rainy days, hunting can still be successful depending on the intensity of the rain. If it is a light rain, hunting from elevated stands or blinds near food sources can be very effective - bears may have to come out of their dens due to the rainfall and search for food in order to stay warm. However, if it is raining heavily, hunting may not be possible as bears will remain in their dens until the storm passes. Additionally, hunting during heavy rain can make firearms or bows dangerous to use due to wet conditions and poor visibility.

On days when it is snowing, hunting can still be successful depending on the amount of snowfall. If it is light snow, hunting from elevated stands or blinds near den sites can be very effective - bears may have to come out of their dens due to the cold temperatures and search for food in order to stay warm. However, hunting during heavy snowfall may not be possible as bears will remain in their dens until the snow passes. Additionally, hunting during heavy snow can make firearms or bows dangerous to use due to wet conditions and poor visibility.

In conclusion, bear hunting presents unique challenges due to its popularity and the environment that they live in. As with all hunting, weather conditions present certain hunting opportunities and challenges. On sunny days hunting can be more successful due to increased activity, on overcast days hunting near food sources is more beneficial, hunting during cold days can be comfortable due to bear's sluggishness, hunting during a light rain can still be productive, but hunting during heavy rains or snowfalls should be avoided. Understanding the weather conditions and how they affect bear hunting will help you increase your chances of success when hunting these majestic animals.

Where to Hunt

Going bear hunting can be an exciting and rewarding experience, as long as you know where to look. There are certain places that bears are more likely to inhabit, making them ideal hunting grounds for those looking to take down a bear. In this section, we will discuss the different areas where bears can be found, the benefits of hunting each place and the techniques that work best in each environment. Keep reading if you want to learn how to increase your chances of success when hunting for bears!

One of the most popular places to find bears is out in fields. Bears tend to like wide-open areas with plenty of room for them to move around and search for food. Hunting these fields provides an excellent opportunity for hunters to spot them from a distance and get close enough for a good shot. The hunting techniques used in fields usually involve stalking or tracking. Stalking involves trying to make your way close to the bear by being quiet, moving slowly and using natural cover like trees and shrubs as camouflage. Tracking involves following the trail of signs left behind by the bear, such as scat, tracks or fur caught on branches.

Another popular hunting ground is woods. Bears tend to inhabit dense forests with plenty of trees that provide protection from predators, shade and food sources like berries and acorns. Hunting in these kinds of places can be very rewarding since bears are often spotted at hunting grounds circling around trees looking for food. When hunting in the woods, hunters should use techniques such as tree stands, stalking and tracking. Tree stands are ideal for hunting since they allow you to get high up into a tree and look down on the bear, giving you an advantage when it comes to getting a good shot.

Another great hunting spot is near water sources or areas with plenty of food sources. Bears tend to gravitate towards these places since they offer them easy access to sustenance. Hunting near these kinds of places can be very rewarding, especially during times of drought when water sources become scarce. The hunting techniques used here involve stalking and baiting. Baiting involves placing bait (usually something sweet like honey) out in the hunting area to lure the bear in. Once the bear is within range, you can then take your shot.

Bear hunting can be a rewarding and exciting experience if you know where to look for them and how to hunt effectively. As discussed above, bears tend to inhabit different kinds of places such as fields, woods and near water and food sources. For each hunting ground there are certain techniques that work best including stalking, tracking and baiting. With some practice and patience, you too could become an expert bear hunter!

Scouting

When scouting for bear, one should pay attention to signs that they may come across while out hunting. These could include tracks, scat, tree rubs and scrapes, den sites and trails made by bears travelling through an area. Identifying these signs helps hunters understand where bears are active so that they can adjust their hunting strategies accordingly. By knowing what type of sign the bear is leaving behind, hunting can become a much more successful endeavor.

Tracks are often the most visible sign that a bear may have passed through an area. Look for tracks with four distinct toes and a concave shape in the middle of the print. Also pay attention to what type of terrain the tracks are on as this can indicate different types of movements and hunting styles for bears.

Scat (droppings) can also be used to find signs of bear activity in an area. Scat will vary in size depending on what the bear has been eating and will contain bones, hair, or other material from its diet. By understanding how different types of scat look like, you'll be able to determine if there is bear activity in an area.

Tree rubs and ground scrapes are also signs that bears have visited a particular area. Tree rubs indicate that the bear has been marking its territory, while scrapes can be found around den sites or food sources where bear may have been foraging for food. Pay attention to the size of the tree rub and look for evidence of claw marks which show that it was made by a bear. Ground scrapes are usually large puddles with disturbed soil, indicating that a bear has stopped there to rest or mark its territory.

Bear dens can also be used as signposts when scouting for hunting locations. Bear dens will vary depending on their species, but they all provide a place of refuge for the bear. Look for large excavations in the ground, often with a pile of sticks or leaves outside it. If a den is being used, it's likely that bears are hunting in the area and you should take extra precautions when hunting close by.

Finally, pay attention to trails that have been made by bears travelling through an area. These trails will be wide and easily recognizable if they have been well-used by multiple animals. By understanding where these trails lead to and from, hunters can understand where the bear may be hunting or seeking food sources.

In conclusion, scouting for bear is essential for successful hunting trips. Paying attention to tracks, scat, tree rubs, ground scrapes, dens and trails can help hunters understand where bear may be hunting and what strategies they should use when hunting. By understanding the signs of bear activity, hunting trips can become much more successful and rewarding.

Bear Decoys

Decoys are often used to attract bears for hunting. A decoy is an imitation of something that the bear thinks it can get a quick meal from, such as a deer fawn. By placing the deer fawn in a highly visible spot, this can draw in hungry bears that may come close enough for you to shoot.

There are various techniques available when setting up a decoy hunting strategy. One method is to place the decoy near openings or trails where bears commonly travel. This gives them easy access and allows them to have plenty of time to observe their potential prey before coming closer. You should also consider putting your hunting stand or blind in an elevated position so you can easily see approaching bears but remain hidden from view until it is time to shoot.

In conclusion, decoys are an effective hunting tactic for bears that can draw them in close enough for a successful shot. The correct placement and timing will help ensure the highest chances of success on your next hunting trip. By understanding which techniques work best for certain hunting scenarios, you'll be able to make the most of each outing and increase your chances of getting a successful bear hunting experience.

Calling Bear

An electronic caller system is a device with a speaker and remote control that plays recorded sounds to attract bears. The most effective call sounds are those of injured animals, such as deer, elk, moose and rabbits. This is because the bear will think an animal is in distress and come hunting for an easy meal.

To effectively use an electronic caller system to hunt bear, it's best to combine calls with decoys. A decoy should be set up in a visible spot at least twenty yards away from your hunting spot. The decoy should mimic the same type of animal sound being played on the electronic caller. Once this is done, remain well-concealed in your hunting spot and wait for the bear to approach.

It's also important to remember that hunting bears with an electronic caller system is a waiting game and it can take quite some time before you see any results. You should be patient and remain still in your hunting spot until the bear comes into view. Additionally, being aware of your surroundings is paramount as you never know when a bear could appear from behind you or very close by.

Overall, hunting with an electronic caller system requires patience and knowledge in order to maximize success. It's best to use calls in combination with a decoy and set up both far away from your hunting spot while keeping an eye out for approaching animals at all times. With practice and careful observation, you will be able to successfully hunting bears with an electronic caller system.

Methods

There are many different techniques for hunting bear that can be utilized depending on the situation, weather and type of area you're hunting in. Some of these techniques include baiting, spot and stalk hunting, and hunting with electronic callers or decoys. Each has its own advantages and disadvantages so it's important to understand which method is best suited to your particular hunting situation.

Baiting bear involves placing bait in an area that they frequent before hunting season begins. This allows the bear to become accustomed to visiting the area when food is available, making hunting much easier. Baiting can be done with food such as sweets or other treats that bear are attracted to. Once the bait has been placed ahead of hunting season, a hunter should then wait in a hunting blind or elevated stand until the bear approach and give them an opportunity for a shot. This method requires patience and time since hunting isn't usually successful on the first trip out. However, it does allow for more precise targeting due to the bear being accustomed to visiting the area with bait.

Spot and stalk hunting is done by slowly walking through wooded areas looking for bear activity such as tracks, scat or rubs from where they have been scratching against trees. Once you have located bear activity, a hunter can then attempt to spot the bear by using binoculars or spotting scopes. This method requires a great deal of experience and patience since it's often difficult to locate bear in their natural habitat. Spot and stalk hunting also requires greater physical effort than hunting in a blind or stand, as it involves slowly walking through the woods searching for bear.

Another popular hunting method is to use electronic callers and decoys to attract bears. By playing recordings of real bear sounds or placing decoys near hunting stands and blinds, hunters can lure bears close enough for an accurate shot. This method allows hunters more freedom of movement since they don't have to remain in a hunting blind or stand. However, it requires a great deal of practice to master the art of using electronic callers and decoys effectively.

Trapping is another hunting method that can be used to catch bears. This is a great way to ensure an accurate shot without having to put in the work of hunting. Trapping involves setting up traps baited with food and waiting for bear to approach them. Once they are inside, the hunters can then take their shot. This method requires a lot of knowledge about bear behavior and habitat as well as patience since it may take some time before the bear approaches the trap.

Bear hunting can be an exciting and rewarding experience if done correctly. While there are many different methods available for hunting bear, it's important to understand which one is best suited for your particular hunting situation. Utilizing the right hunting methods and techniques can ensure that you have a successful hunting experience.

Where to Shoot Bear

When hunting bear, it is important to know where to aim for the quickest and most humane kill. Taking a clean shot is essential for ensuring the animal does not suffer and that as much meat can be used from the animal as possible. The heart and lungs are typically considered the best place to aim because they will result in an immediate and painless death, causing minimal damage to other parts of the animal's body. In this section of our book, we will explain why aiming for the heart and lungs is often recommended when hunting bear.

The heart and lungs make up a large area on an bear's chest cavity which makes them easy targets when hunting. Bear have thick hides that can be difficult to penetrate with hunting arrows or bullets, so it is ideal to aim for this larger area rather than attempting a more precise shot. The heart and lungs are positioned close together in the bear's body, so when shooting an arrow or bullet into this area of the chest cavity, it is highly likely both organs will be hit.

When aiming for the heart and lungs, death should occur shortly after impact due to a lack of oxygen to the brain. This result gives hunters peace of mind knowing the animal has been killed quickly and humanely. In addition, hunting arrows or bullets will typically pass through the chest cavity with minimal damage to other parts of the body, allowing hunting enthusiasts to make the most of their hunting experience.

Tracking Bear After the Shot

In hunting, it is not always a guarantee that an animal will die immediately where you shot it and in order to find your bear, you need to track the animal's path. Tracking can often be a process requiring patience and focus as well as skillful observation.

Before starting to track, it is important to wait at least half an hour before searching for the animal. This gives enough time for the animal to bleed out and die naturally so that they do not run away when approached. It also allows time to check if another one was following the first one which may give you an opportunity to shoot a second target.

The tracking process itself begins at the spot where the animal was shot. It is important to look for clues such as blood spots, broken leaves and branches which can indicate a change in direction of the animal's path. Differentiating between fresh and old blood is also important since if you see older or dried up blood stains, it means that you may be on a wrong trail. When hunting bigger game animals like bear, it is essential to mark your last location with a marker such as fabric scraps or pieces of paper so that you can start from that point again in case you lose the trail.

It is also important to be aware of subtle differences in the appearance of blood depending on where and how deeply you hit an animal. For example, if you hit an bear in its vital organs, the blood will be bright red and flow faster compared to a situation when you just graze it on its side. With more experience you know how to accurately read these signs.

In order to track an bear successfully after shooting it, patience and observational skills are essential in hunting. It also involves deducing where the animal has gone based on subtle changes of direction indicated by physical markers left behind as well as being able to tell apart fresh from old blood trails. All of this requires practice which is why hunting with experienced instructors is recommended for those who wish to learn the proper way. With time and practice, one can become a successful bear hunting.

Cleaning Your Bear

Once you have harvested an bear, there is still more work to be done: cleaning and field dressing it. Field dressing an bear requires some specific hunting equipment like disposable plastic gloves, a hunting knife with a sharp blade, and rope or twine.

When cleaning your game, it is important that you wear the protective gloves at all times to prevent any bacterial contamination of the meat. Always remember to use caution when dealing with hunting knives; they can be dangerous if not handled properly.

The first step in field dressing an bear is cutting along the chest plate from the front of the bear through the belly. You need to be careful and not cut too deep, as this will damage the internal organs and limit the amount of usable meat. Once you have successfully made this incision, you can use your hunting knife to separate the skin from the body in a downward motion. Now that you have exposed the internal organs, it is time to remove them by either pulling or cutting them away with care.

After removing all of the entrails, it is time to bring your game out of the woods. If necessary, you should quarter out your bear for easier transport. Quartering involves cutting off both front legs at the shoulder, and then the hind legs at the hip joints. You can use twine or rope to tie up the quarters for transport. Once you are home, it is easy to finish processing your bear by removing all of the meat from the bones.

Field dressing an bear properly requires some skill and knowledge about hunting techniques. But with patience and practice, anyone can learn how to clean their game successfully in order to get the most out of their hunting experience. It is important that you dispose of remains in a safe manner and not to leave them out in the open. As long as you take the proper precautions, hunting bear can be an enjoyable experience for everyone involved.

Cooking Your Game

After taking down a bear, hunters must decide how to cook it. Bear meat is incredibly versatile and can be prepared in a variety of ways, each with its own distinct flavor and texture. Whether grilling, stewing, pan-frying or transforming the bear into jerky or hot dogs, there are many options available. In this section we will explore the different ways bear can be cooked, as well as discuss some of the nutritional benefits that come along with incorporating bear into your diet.

Stewing

The most common way to prepare bear meat is by stewing the cuts in liquid until they become tender enough to eat. To make a stew out of bear, simply place cubed bear meat into a bay leaf and garlic-flavored broth. Simmer the stew for 2-3 hours until the bear is tender. Serve with cooked potatoes and carrots for a hearty meal.

Grilling

The best way to enjoy bear steak is by grilling it on high heat. Coat the steak with olive oil, garlic and rosemary then season generously with salt and pepper. Place onto a hot grill surface for about 4 minutes per side or until desired doneness has been reached. Bear steaks are also delicious when served alongside grilled vegetables such as corn, zucchini or bell peppers.

Shredded Bear

Another great way to prepare bear meat is by shredding it and using it in your favorite tacos or burritos. To make shredded bear, first simmer the cubed bear meat until tender. Once cooked, shred the bear with two forks then add a variety of seasonings such as smoked paprika, chili powder and cumin to give it an extra kick of flavor. Add the shredded bear to your favorite shell for an easy and delicious meal.

Ground Bear

For those not wanting to eat large chunks of bear meat, ground bear is another great way to enjoy the taste without having to deal with bigger cuts. To make ground bear, simply place cubed or chopped pieces into a food processor and pulse until the desired consistency has been reached. Ground bear can be used like any other ground beef or pork, and can be used in burgers, tacos, or even chili.

Pan Frying

For a quick and easy meal, pan-fry cubed bear meat with oil and garlic until golden brown. The bear cubes can be served with potatoes and a side of vegetables for a delicious dinner. Alternatively, the bear cubes can also be diced down into small pieces then tossed into stir fry dishes along with other ingredients such as broccoli, bell peppers and mushrooms for an Asian-inspired dish.

Jerky/Sausage/Hot Dogs

To reduce any gamy taste that may come from bear meat, many people opt to turn it into jerky or sausage. When making these items out of bear meat it is usually mixed with pork, spices and other flavorings to make it taste closer to a standard beef or pork product. Bear jerky can be enjoyed as a snack on its own or used in sandwiches for added flavor and texture. Sausage made from bear meat can be served up for breakfast, lunch or dinner, while hot dogs are also an easy way to add some bear into your diet.

Nutritional Benefits

In addition to being delicious, bear meat has numerous nutritional benefits that may surprise you. It is loaded with protein and is considered to be one of the leanest sources of game meat available today. Bear contains more iron than beef and is also rich in Vitamin B-12 which helps keep energy levels up throughout the day. Eating bear is also a great way to get more Omega-3s into your diet, as bear meat contains higher amounts of these fatty acids than beef or pork.

The Environment and You

Being a good sportsperson when hunting bear involves more than just hunting responsibly. It also means taking care of the land and wildlife around you, being respectful of other hunters, and even giving back to organizations that protect bear hunting grounds. To be an ethical hunter is to accept responsibility for your actions before, during, and after your hunting trips. Read on to learn more about what it takes to be a good sportsperson while hunting bear!

One way you can show respect for the environment while hunting bear is by cleaning up any litter or debris left behind by others in the hunting ground. This includes things like empty cans or bottles, food wrappers, and hunting equipment or clothing that have been left behind. By ensuring that hunting grounds are free of litter and debris, you not only help to protect bear hunting grounds but also ensure that other hunters can enjoy their hunting trips in a clean environment.

When hunting bear, it is important to be respectful of other hunters in the area by following local hunting regulations and not interfering with another hunter's hunt. This means staying on designated trails, hunting only during designated hours, and avoiding areas where other hunters are actively hunting. Show respect for other hunters by keeping your distance and being mindful of your actions while in the hunting ground.

In addition to hunting responsibly and respecting other hunters, you can also show your support for bear hunting by joining or donating to organizations that focus on wildlife management programs. These organizations work to protect hunting grounds and ensure that bear hunting can be enjoyed for years to come. By becoming involved with these organizations, you can help promote responsible hunting practices and conservation of hunting grounds.

Being a good sportsperson while hunting bear involves more than just hunting responsibly. It also means taking care of the land and wildlife around you, being respectful of other hunters in the area, and giving back to organizations that protect bear hunting grounds. Taking the time to follow these tips will ensure that all hunting trips are enjoyable and responsible.

Recap

Hunting for bears is an exciting and rewarding experience that can be enjoyed by kids of all ages. And now that you've read this book, you know just how to do it! You should feel confident in your hunting abilities and ready to get out there and explore the great outdoors.

Not only is bear hunting fun, but it also teaches kids valuable skills. Kids learn important hunting skills such as tracking, weapon safety, patience and respect for nature while hunting. Not to mention, hunting can promote physical activity which is always beneficial for kids. Spending time outdoors helps reduce stress levels while building confidence at the same time.

So if you are looking for a thrilling outdoor activity to enjoy with family or friends, bear hunting is an excellent choice. With the right preparation and safety measures in place, you can have a safe and successful hunting trip every time.

Happy hunting!